* 1,000,000 *

Free E-Books

@

www . Forgotten Books . org

* Alchemy *

The Secret is Revealed

@

www.TheBookofAquarius.com

D1319253

Poems of Reflection

By

Ella Wheeler Wilcox

Published by Forgotten Books 2012

PIBN 1000175025

Copyright © 2012 Forgotten Books
www.forgottenbooks.org

POEMS
of
REFLECTION

by

ELLA WHEELER WILCOX

POEMS OF
POEMS OF

OUT OF THE DEPTHS

Copyright 1905.

M. A. Donohue & C

PS
3312
P77

CONTENTS.

CONTENTS.

CONTENTS.

BOHEMIA.

Bohemia, o'er thy unatlassed borders
  How many cross, with half-reluctant feet,
And unformed fears of dangers and disorders,
  To find delights, more wholesome and more sweet
  Than ever yet were known to the "*elite.*"

Herein can dwell no pretence and no seeming;
  No stilted pride thrives in this atmosphere,
Which stimulates a tendency to dreaming.
  The shores of the ideal world, from here,
  Seem sometimes to be tangible and near.

We have no use for formal codes of fashion;
  No "Etiquette of Courts" we emulate;
We know it needs sincerity and passion
  To carry out the plans of God, or fate;
  We do not strive to seem inanimate.

We call no time lost that we give to pleasure;
  Life's hurrying river speeds to Death's great
      sea;
We cast out no vain plummet-line to measure
  Imagined depths of that unknown To Be,
  But grasp the *Now,* and fill it full of glee.

All creeds have room here, and we all together
  Devoutly worship at Art's sacred shrine;
But he who dwells once in thy golden weather,
  Bohemia—sweet, lovely land of mine—
  Can find no joy outside thy border-line.

PENALTY.

Because of the fullness of what I had,
    All that I have seems poor and vain.
If I had not been happy, I were not sad—
    Tho' my salt is savorless, why complain?

From the ripe perfection of what was mine,
    All that is mine seems worse than naught;
Yet I know, as I sit in the dark and pine,
    No cup could be drained which had not been
      fraught.

From the throb and thrill of a day that was,
    The day that now is seems dull with gloom;
Yet I bear the dullness and darkness, because
    'Tis but the reaction of glow and bloom.

From the royal feast that of old was spread
    I am starved on the diet that now is mine;
Yet, I could not turn hungry from water and bread
    If I had not been sated on fruit and wine.

see p. 87  **LIFE.**

An infant—wailing in nameless fear;
  A shadow, perchance, in the quiet room,
Or the hum of an insect flying near,
  Or the screech owl's cry in the outer gloom.

A little child on the sun-checked floor;
  A broken toy, and a tear-stained face;
A young life clouded, a young heart sore,
  And the great clock, Time, ticks on apace.

A maiden weeping in bitter pain;
  Two white hands clasped on an aching brow;
A blighted faith, and a fond hope slain,
  A shattered trust, and a broken vow.

A matron holding a baby's shoe;
  The hot tears gather and fall at will,
On the knotted ribbon of white and blue,
  For the foot that wore it is cold and still.

 An aged woman upon her bed,
  Worn and wearied, and poor and old;

Longing to rest with the happy dead;
And thus the story of life is told.

Where is the season of careless glee;
Where is the moment that holds no pain,
Life has its crosses from infancy
Down to the grave, and its hopes are vain.

LINES FROM "MAURINE."

I'd rather have my verses win
  A place in common peoples' hearts,
Who, toiling through the strife and din
  Of life's great thoroughfares, and marts.

May read some line my hand has penned;
  Some simple verse, not fine, or grand,
  But what their hearts can understand
And hold me henceforth as a friend,—

I'd rather win *such* quiet fame
  Than by some fine thought, polished so
  But those of learned minds would know,
  Just what the meaning of my song,—
To have the critics sound my name
  In high-flown praises, loud and long.

I sing not for the critic's ear,
But for the masses. If they hear,
Despite the turmoil, noise and strife
Some least low note that gladdens life,
I shall be wholly satisfied,
Though critics to the end deride.

WHEN.

I dwell in the western inland,
   Afar from the sounding sea,
But I seem to hear it sobbing
   And calling aloud to me,
And my heart cries out for the ocean
   As a child for its mother's breast,
And I long to lie on its waters
   And be lulled in its arms to rest.

I can close my eyes and fancy
   That I hear its mighty roar,
And I see its blue waves splashing
   And plunging against the shore;
And the white foam caps the billow,
   And the sea-gulls wheel and cry,
And the cool wild wind is blowing
   And the ships go sailing by.

Oh, wonderful, mighty ocean!
   When shall I ever stand,
Where my heart has gone already,
   There on thy gleaming strand!

When shall I ever wander
  Away from this inland west,
And stand by thy side, dear ocean,
  And rock on thy heaving breast?

ONLY DREAMS.

A maiden sat in the sunset glow
Of the shadowy, beautiful Long Ago,
   That we see through a mist of tears.
She sat and dreamed, with lips apart,
With thoughtful eyes and a beating heart,
   Of the mystical future years;
And brighter far than the sunset skies
Was the vision seen by the maiden's eyes.

There were castles built of the summer air,
And beautiful voices were singing there,
   In a soft and floating strain.
There were skies of azure and fields of green,
With never a cloud to come between,
   And never a thought of pain;
There was music, sweet as the silvery notes
That flow from a score of thrushes' throats.

There were hands to clasp with a loving hold;
There were lips to kiss, and eyes that told
   More than the lips could say.
And all of the faces she loved were there,

With their snowy brows untouched by care,
  And locks that were never gray.
And Love was the melody each heart beat,
And the beautiful vision was all complete.

But the castles built of the summer wind
I have vainly sought. I only find
  Shadows, all grim and cold;—
For I was the maiden who thought to see
Into the future years,—Ah, me!
  And I am gray and old.
My dream of earth was as fair and bright
As my hope of heaven is to-night.

Dreams are but dreams at the very best,
And the friends I loved lay down to rest
  With their faces hid away.
They had furrowed brows and snowy hair,
And they willingly laid their burdens where
  Mine shall be laid one day.
A shadow came over my vision scene
As the clouds of sorrow came in between.

The hands that I thought to clasp are crossed,
The lips and the beautiful eyes are lost,
  And I seek them all in vain.
The gushes of melody, sweet and clear,

And the floating voices, I do not hear,
  But only a sob of pain;
And the beating hearts have paused to rest,
Ah! dreams are but dreams at the very best.

"IN THE NIGHT."

In the silent midnight watches,
    When the earth was wrapped in gloom,
And the grim and awful darkness
    Crept unbidden to my room,
On the solemn, deathly stillness
    Of the night there broke a sound
Like ten million wailing voices,
    Crying loudly from the ground.

From ten million graves, came voices
    East and west and north and south.
Leagues apart, and yet together
    Spake they, e'en as with one mouth.
"Men and women, men and women,"
    Cried these voices from the ground,
And the very earth was shaken
    With the strange and awful sound.

"Ye who weep in selfish sorrow,
    Ye who laugh in selfish mirth,
Hark! and listen for a moment
    To the voices from the earth.

Wake, and listen, ye who slumber.
　　Pause, and listen, ye who feast,
To the warning of the voices
　　From the graves in west and east.

"We, the victims of a demon, *p. 23*
　　We, who one, and each, and all,
Can cry out before high Heaven,
　　We are slain by Alcohol.
We would warn you, youths and maidens,
　　From the path that we have trod.
From the path that leads to ruin,
　　And away from Peace and God.

"We, the millions who have fallen,
　　Warn you from the ruddy glow
Of the wine in silver goblets,
　　For destruction lies below,
Wine and gin, and rum and brandy,
　　Whiskey, cider, ale and beer:
These have slain us, and destroyed us—
　　These the foes that brought us here.

"You are safe, you say? ah, Heaven!
　　So we said, and drank, and died,
We are safe, we proudly boasted,
　　Yet we sunk down in the tide.

There is never any safety
From the snares of Alcohol,
For the youth who looks on liquor,
Tastes, or handles it at all.

"We beseech you, men and women,
Fathers, Mothers, Husbands, Wives,
To arise and slay the demon
That is threatening dear one's lives.
Do not preach of moderation
To your children, for alas!
There is not a foe more subtle
Than the fateful Social Glass.

"Thoughtless mother, wife or sister,
Dash that poison cup away!
He, the husband, son, or brother,
Who so gaily sips to-day,
May to-morrow stagger homeward,
Jeered and scorned by sober men.
Would you smile upon him proudly--
Would you say 'I did it'—then?

"Ah! a vast and mighty number
Of the drunkards in all lands
Take the first step to destruction
Led by white and fragile hands.

Every smile you give the wine-cup,
  Every glance, oh lady fair,
Like a spade digs down, and hollows
Out, a drunkard's grave, somewhere.

"Men in office, men in power:
  Will you let this demon wild
Stalk unfettered through the nation,
  Slaying woman, man, and child?
Oh, arouse, ye listless mortals!
  There is work for every one!
We have warned you of your danger;
  We have spoken—we have done!"

Round about me fell the silence
  Of the solemn night, once more,
And I heard the quiet ticking
  Of the clock outside my door.
It was not a dreamer's fancy—
  Not a romance of my brain—
But the warning of the victims
  That Old Alcohol had slain.

CONTENTMENT.

If any line that I ever penned,
　　Or any word I have spoken,
Has comforted heart, of foe or friend—
　　In any way, why my life, I'll say
Has reaped the reward of labor.
　　If aught I have said, or written, has made
Gladder the heart o' my neighbor.

If any deed that I ever did
　　Lightened a sad heart's sorrow,
If I have lifted a drooping lid
　　Up to the bright to-morrow,
Though the world knows not, nor gives me a
　　　thought,
　　Nor ever can know, nor praise me.
Yet still I shall say, to my heart alway,
　　That my life, and labor repays me.

If in any way I have helped a soul,
　　Or given a spirit pleasure,
Then my cup of joy, I shall think is full
　　With an overflowing measure.

Though never an eye, but the one on high
  Looks on my kindly action,
Yet, oh my heart, we shall think of our part
  In the drama, with satisfaction.

A NEW YEAR'S GREETING TO THE CITY OF THE LAKES.

I said "I will write a greeting,
  To the City of the Lakes,
Write, while the city sleepeth,
  And sing it when it wakes.

"To this fair, and blessed city,
  That the glad New Year doth bring
Its best, and its sweetest treasure,
  Its choicest offering.

"It brings to our joyful Nation,
  The boon of Peace again,
The fields are white, not scarlet,
  With the death-blood of the slain.

"And not with the sounds of sobbing,
  Do we usher in the year,
Not with hand clasps, and partings,
  But with goodly mirth and cheer.

"And brother shall meet with brother,
  In peace, from North to South,
And 'I wish you a happy New Year,'
  Shall echo from mouth to mouth.

"And there shall be feast, and revel,
  In many a home, to-day,
(God grant that the wine be banished
  From every board away.)

"Thank God for his righteous goodness,
  For a land not red with strife—
Thank God for the New Year's blessing,
  Thank God for the boon of life.

"Oh! beautiful white-robed city,
  Asleep in the arms of Lakes,
I write me a song while it slumbers,
  And I'll sing me a song when it wakes."

And thus while I dreamed, and pondered,
  O'er the glad song I would sing,
Lo! I saw the sun was rising,
  And my muse had taken wing.

MOTHER'S LOSS.

If I could clasp my little babe
  Upon my breast to-night,
I would not mind the blowing wind
  That shrieketh in affright.
Oh, my lost babe! my little babe,
  My babe with dreamful eyes;
Thy bed is cold; and night wind bold
  Shrieks woeful lullabies.

My breast is softer than the sod;
  This room, with lighter hearth,
Is better place for thy sweet face
  Than frozen mother earth.
Oh, my babe! oh, my lost babe!
  Oh, babe with waxen hands.
I want thee so, I need thee so—
  Come from thy mystic lands!

No love that, like a mother's, fills
 ˙ Each corner of the heart;
No loss like hers, that rends, and chills,
  And tears the soul apart.
Oh, babe—my babe, my helpless babe!
  I miss thy little form.
Would I might creep where thou dost sleep,
  And clasp thee through the storm.

I hold thy pillow to my breast,
  To bring a vague relief;
I sing the songs that soothed thy rest—
  Ah me! no cheating grief.
My breathing babe! my sobbing babe!
  I miss thy plaintiff moan,
I cannot hear—thou art not near—
  My little one, my own.

Thy father sleeps. He mourns thy loss,
  But little fathers know
The pain that makes a mother toss
  Through sleepless nights of woe.
My clinging babe! my nursing babe!
  What knows thy father—man—
How my breasts miss thy lips soft kiss—
  None but a mother can.
Worn out, I sleep; I wake—I weep—
  I sleep—hush, hush, my dear;
Sweet lamb, fear not—Oh, God! I thought—
  I thought my babe was here.

THE WOMEN.

See the women—pallid women, of our land!
See them fainting, dying, dead, on every hand!
  See them sinking 'neath a weight
  Far more burdensome than Fate
Ever placed upon poor human beings' backs.
  See them falling as they go—
  By their own hands burdened so—
Paling, failing, sighing, dying, on their tracks!

See the women—ghastly women, on the streets!
With their corset-tortured waists, and pinched up
    feet!
  Hearts and lungs all out of place,
  Whalebone forms devoid of grace;
Faces pallid, robbed of Nature's rosy bloom;
  Purple-lidded eyes that tell,
  With a language known too well,
Of the sick-room, death-bed, coffin, pall and tomb.

See the women—sickly women, everywhere,
See the cruel, killing dresses that they wear!
  Bearing round those pounds of jet,
  Can you wonder that they fret,

Pale, and pine, and fall the victims of decay?
　Is it strange the blooming maid,
　All so soon should droop and fade—
Like a beast of burden burdened, day on day?

See the women and their dresses as they go,
Trimmed and retrimmed, line on line and row on
　　row;
　Hanging over fragile hips,
　Driving color from the lips,
Dragging down their foolish wearers to the grave!
　Suicide, and nothing less,
　In this awful style of dress!
Who shall rise to women's rescue, who shall save?

See the women—foolish women, dying fast;
What have all their trimmed-up dresses brought
　　at last?
　Worry, pain, disease and death,
　Loss of bloom and gasping breath;
Doctors' bill, and golden hours thrown away.
　They have bartered off for these
　Beauty, comfort, health and ease—
All to ape the fleeting fashion of a day.

LEAN DOWN AND LIFT ME HIGHER.

Lean down and lift me higher, Josephine;
From the eternal hills hast thou not seen;
How I do strive for heights? but lacking wings,
I cannot grasp at once these better things,
To which I in my inmost soul aspire,
    Lean down and lift me higher.

I grope along—not desolate or sad,
For youth and hope and health all keep me glad;
But too bright sunlight sometimes makes us blind,
And I do grope for heights I cannot find;
O! thou must know my one supreme desire.
    Lean down and lift me higher.

Not long ago we trod the selfsame way;
Thou knewest how from day to fleeting day;
Our souls were vexed with trifles, and our feet
Were lured aside to by-paths that seemed sweet,
But only served to hinder and to tire.
    Lean down and lift me higher.

Thou hast gone onward to the heights serene
And left me here, my loved one, Josephine.

I am content to stay until the end,
For life is full of promise; but, my friend,
Canst thou not help me in my best desire?
    O! lean and lift me higher.

Frail tho' thou wert, thou hast grown strong and
    wise,
And quick to understand and sympathize
With all a full soul's needs. It must be so;
Thy year with God hath made thee great, I know.
Thou must see how I struggle and aspire;
O warm me with a breath of heavenly fire.
    And lean and lift me higher.

A TRIBUTE TO VINNIE REAM.

All hail to Vinnie Ream!
  Wisconsin's artist daughter,
Who stands to-day crowned with the fame
  Her noble work has brought her.
Lift up your brows, hills of the West,
  And tell the winds the story,
How she, our fairest, and our best,
  Has climbed the heights of glory.

Three cheers for Vinnie Ream!
  Who fought with tribulation,
And brought from death, to lasting life,
  The martyr of our Nation.
Oh, Spite and Envy, flee in shame!
  And hide your head, black Malice!
She sips, to-day, the sweets of Fame,
  From Fame's emblazoned chalice.

Thank God for Vinnie Ream!
  The peerless Badger maiden,
Who stands a nation's pride, to-day
  With a nation's honors laden.

Ay! crown her Queen at every feast,
  And strew her path with flowers,
Ye people of the South and East,
  But remember, she is ours!

Bring gifts to Vinnie Ream!
  I have no gift to offer,
Only a little gift of song,
  And that I humbly proffer;—
Only this little gift to lay
  Before Columbia's daughter,
Who stands crowned with the fame, to-day,
  That her noble work has brought her.

THE LITTLE BIRD.

The father sits in his lonely room,
  Outside sings a little bird.
But the shadows are laden with death and gloom,
  And the song is all unheard.
The father's heart is the home of sorrow;
  His breast is the seat of grief!
Who will hunt the paper for him on the morrow—
  Who will bring him sweet relief
From wearing thought with innocent chat?
Who will find his slippers and bring his hat?
     Still the little bird sings
     And flutters her wings;
The refrain of her song is, "God knows best!
He giveth his little children rest."
What can she know of these sorrowful things?

The mother sits by the desolate hearth,
  And weeps o'er a vacant chair.
Sorrow has taken the place of mirth—
  Joy has resigned to despair.
Bitter the cup the mother is drinking,
  So bitter the tear-drops start.
Sad are the thoughts the mother is thinking—
  Oh, they will break her heart.

Who will run on errands, and romp and play,
And mimic the robins the livelong day?
     Still the little bird sings
     And flutters her wings;
"God reigns in heaven, and He will keep
The dear little children that fall asleep."
What can she know of these sorrowful things?

Grandmother sits by the open door,
   And her tears fall down like rain.
Was there ever a household so sad before,
   Will it ever be glad again?
Many unwelcome thoughts come flitting
   Into the granddame's mind.
Who will take up the stitches she drops in knitting?
   Who will her snuff-box find?
Who'll bring her glasses, and wheel her chair,
And tie her kerchief, and comb her hair?
     Still the little bird sings
     And flutters her wings;
"God above doeth all things well, See p. 47
I sang it the same when my nestlings fell."
Ah! this knows the bird of these sorrowful things.

"VAMPIRES."

Lo! here's another corpse exhumed!
 Another Poet, disinterred!
Sensation cried, "Dig up the grave,
 And let the dust be hoed and stirred,
And bring the bones of Shakespeare out!
'Twill edify the throng, no doubt!

"The Byron scandal has grown old;
 That rare tit-bit is flat and stale.
The throng is gaping for more food;
 We need a new Sensation tale;
Old Shakespeare sleeps too well, and sound;
Tear off the shroud—dig up the ground.

"We have exhumed poor 'Raven Poe,'
 And proved beyond the shade of doubt,
He saw no raven, after all.
 Now trot the bones of Shakespeare out!
Byron, and Poe, and Shakespeare—good!
Who shall we serve up next, for food?"

And who? say I. Oh, seers of earth,
 What corpse comes next? I daily look

To see if some sage hasn't proved
　　That Jones or Brown wrote Lalla Rookh.
Or Blifkins lent his brains to Moore,
Who was a plagiarist and boor!

Sensation, have your servants out—
Let them be watchful and alert;
We'll need a new discovery soon.
　　Tell them to dig about the dirt,
And tear off Keats' or Shelley's shroud,
To please and edify the crowd.

DYING.

Let my head lie on your shoulder   *p24, p.22*

~~Let me lie upon your breast,~~
  Lift me up, and let me twine
  with my love & make me bolder
~~Round your neck my arms, and rest~~
  With your cheek laid close to mine.
  Give me strength to see the morrow
~~Kiss me, kiss me tenderly;~~
  I am dying now, you know;
  Though you feel me slipping from you
~~Though you feel no love for me,~~
  Clasp me, kiss me, ~~ere~~ *when* I go.

I have lingered many years,
  For a moment, love, like this;
Oh! my darling! let no tears
  Mar this drop of earthly bliss;
Do not weep because you know
  I am dropping off to rest;
I am very glad to go,
  Life was wearisome at best.

I have loved you, oh, so long,
  Seeing, knowing, in my brain,
That my love was wild and wrong,
  Unrequitted, hopeless, vain;

Was it weak, unwomanly,
　Thus to shrine you in my heart?
Oh! I struggled frantically—
　Bade your image to depart.

There are hearts that love will pierce,
　Then depart, and die at will;
Such as mine burns long and fierce,
　Till the heart is cold and still,
Dropping, sinking off to rest,
　Fearing naught of pain or strife:
Kiss me—clasp me to your breast,
　This is all I ask of life.

THE KING AND SIREN.

The harsh King—Winter—sat upon the hills,
  And reigned and ruled the earth right royally.
He locked the rivers, lakes, and all the rills—
  "I am no puny, maudlin king," quoth he,
"But a stern monarch, born to rule, and reign;
  And I'll show my power to the end.
The Summer's flowery retinue I've slain,
  And taken the bold free North Wind for my
    friend.

"Spring, Summer, Autumn—feeble queens they
    were,
  With their vast troops of flowers, birds and bees,
Soft winds, that made the long green grasses stir—
  They lost their own identity in things like these!
I scorn them all! nay, I defy them all!
  And none can wrest the sceptre from my hand.
The trusty North Wind answers to my call,
  And breathes his icy breath upon the land."

The Siren—South Wind—listening the while,
  Now floated airily across the lea.
"Oh King!" she cried, with tender tone and smile,
  "I come to do all homage unto thee.

In all the sunny region, whence I came,
   I find none like thee, King, so brave and grand!
Thine is a well deserved, unrivaled fame;
   I kiss, in awe, dear King, thy cold white hand.''

Her words were pleasing, and most fair her face.
   He listened wrapt, to her soft-whispered praise.
She nestled nearer, in her Siren grace.
   ''Dear King,'' she said, ''henceforth my voice
     shall raise
But songs of thy unrivaled splendor! Lo!
   How white thy brow is! How thy garments
     shine!
I tremble 'neath thy beaming glance, for Oh,
   Thy wondrous beauty mak'st thee seem divine.''

The rain King listened, in a trance of bliss,
   To this most sweet-voiced Siren from the South,
She nestled close, and pressed a lingering kiss
   Upon the stern white pallor of his mouth.
She hung upon his breast, she pressed his cheek,
   And he was nothing loath to hold her there,
While she such tender, loving words did speak,
   And combed his white locks with her fingers
     fair.

And so she bound him, in her Siren wiles,
   And stole his strength, with every kiss she gave,
And stabbed him through and through, with tender
     smiles,
   And with her loving words, she dug his grave;

And then she left him, old, and weak, and blind,
  And unlocked all the rivers, lakes, and rills,
While the queen Spring, with her whole troop,
    behind,
  Of flowers, and birds, and bees, came o'er the
    hills.

SUNSHINE AND SHADOW.

Life has its shadows, as well as its sun;
   Its lights and its shades, all twined together.
I tried to single them out, one by one,
   Single and count them, determining whether
There was less blue than there was gray,
And more of the deep night than of the day.
But dear me, dear me, my task's but begun,
And I am not half way into the sun.

For the longer I look on the bright side of earth.
   The more of the beautiful do I discover;
And really, I never knew what life was worth
   Till I searched the wide storehouse of happiness
     over.
It is filled from the cellar well up to the skies,
With things meant to gladden the heart and the
     eyes.
The doors are unlocked, you can enter each room,
That lies like a beautiful garden in bloom.

Yet life has its shadow, as well as its sun;
   Earth has its storehouse of joy and of sorrow.

But the first is so wide—and my task's but begun—
  That the last must be left for a far distant
    morrow.
I will count up the blessings God gave in a row,
But dear me! when I get through them, I know
I shall have little time left for the rest,
For life is a swift-flowing river at best.

see p. 37

"WHATEVER IS—IS BEST."

see p. 21 Courage
Crowell "What-
ever is, is best"

I know, as my life grows older,
  And mine eyes have clearer sight—
That under each rank Wrong, somewhere,
  There lies the root of Right.
That each sorrow has its purpose—
  By the sorrowing oft unguessed,
But as sure as the Sun brings morning,
  Whatever is, is best.

I know that each sinful action,
  As sure as the night brings shade,
Is sometime, somewhere, punished,
  Tho' the hour be long delayed.
I know that the soul is aided
  Sometimes by the heart's unrest,
And to grow, means often to suffer—
  But whatever is, is best.

I know there are no errors,
  In the great Eternal plan,
And all things work together
  For the final good of man.

And I know when my soul speeds onward
In the grand, Eternal quest,
I shall say, as I look back earthward,
Whatever is, is best.

TRANSPLANTED.

Where the grim old "Mount of Lamentation"
  Lifts up its summit like some great dome,
I list for the voices of Inspiration
  That rang o'er the meadows and hills of home.
I catch sweet sounds, but I am not near them,
  There are vast, vague oceans between us rolled;
Or it may be my heart is too full to hear them
  With the eager ear that it lent of old.

It is full of the joy of to-day—and to-morrow,
  Which smiles with a promise of fresh delight;
And yet my honey is galled with sorrow
  As I think of the loved ones out of sight.
I wonder so soon if the dear old places
  Are growing used to my absent feet,
I wonder if newer and fairer faces
  To the hearts that housed me seem just as sweet.

I know on the world's great field of battle
  When a comrade falls out how the ranks close in;
The strife goes on with its rush and rattle,
  And who can tell where he late has been?

But through life a grafted vine I may wind me
 About old Eastern homes at length,
The roots of love that I left behind me
 In Western soil will keep their strength.
Though dear grows the "Mount of Lamentation."
 And dear the ocean, and dear the shore,
I shall love the land of my Inspiration,
 Its lakes, its valleys, its *tried hearts*, more.

WORLDLY WISDOM.

If it were in my dead Past's power
   To let my Present bask
In some lost pleasure for an hour,
   This is the boon I'd ask:

Re-pedestal from out the dust
   Where long ago 'twas hurled,
My beautiful incautious trust
   In this unworthy world.

The symbol of my own soul's truth—
   I saw it go with tears—
The sweet unwisdom of my youth—
   That vanished with the years.

Since knowledge brings us only grief,
   I would return again
To happy ignorance and belief
   In motives and in men.

For worldly wisdom learned in pain
   Is in itself a cross,
Significant mayhap of gain,
   Yet sign of saddest loss.

NEW ORLEANS, 1885.

A queen of indolence and idle grace,
　　Robed in the remnants of a costly gown,
She turns the languor of her lovely face
　　Upon Progression, with a lazy frown.
Her throne is built upon a marshy down;
　　Malarial mosses wreathe her, like old lace.
With thin, crossed feet, unshod, and bare and
　　　brown,
　　She sits indifferent to the world's swift race.

Across the seas there stalks an ogre grim.
　　Too listless, she, for even Fear's alarms,
　　　While frightened nations rally in defense,
She lifts her smiling creole eyes to him,
　　And, reaching out her shapely, unwashed arms,
　　　She clasps her rightful lover—Pestilence.

THE ROOM BENEATH THE RAFTERS.

Sometimes when I have dropped asleep,
  Draped in a soft luxurious gloom,
Across my drowsy mind will creep
  The memory of another room,
Where resinous knots in roof boards made
A frescoing of light and shade,
And sighing poplars brushed their leaves
Against the humbly sloping eaves.

Again I fancy in my dreams
  I'm lying in my trundle-bed.
I seem to see the bare old beams
  And unhewn rafters overhead;
The hornet's shrill falsetto hum
I hear again, and see him come
Forth from his mud-walled hanging house,
Dressed in his black and yellow blouse.

There, summer dawns, in sleep I stirred,
  And wove into my fair dream's woof
The chattering of a martin bird,
  Or rain-drops pattering on the roof.

Or, half awake, and half in fear,
I saw the spider spinning near
His pretty çastle, where the fly
Should come to ruin by and by.

And there I fashioned from my brain
    Youth's shining structures in the air,
I did not wholly build in vain,
    For some were lasting, firm and fair.
And I am one who lives to say
My life has held more good than gray,
And that the splendor of the real
Surpassed my early dream's ideal.

But still I love to wander back
    To that old time, and that old place;
To thread my way o'er Memory's track,
    And catch the early morning's grace
In that quaint room beneath the rafter,
That echoed to my childish laughter;
To dream again the dreams that grew
More beautiful as they came true.

MY COMRADE.

Out from my window westward
　I turn full oft my face;
But the mountains rebuke the vision
　That would encompass space;
They lift their lofty foreheads
　To the kiss of the clouds above,
And ask, "With all our glory,
　Can we not win your love?"

I answer, "No, oh mountains!
　I see that you are grand;
But you have not the breadth and beauty
　Of the fields in my own land;
You narrow my range of vision
　And you even shut from me
The voice of my old comrade,
　The West Wind wild and free."

But to-day I climbed the mountains
　On the back of a snow-white steed,
And the West Wind came to greet me—
　He flew on the wings of speed.

His charger, and mine that bore me,
    Went gaily neck to neck.
Till the town in the valley below us
    Looked like a small, dark speck.

And oh! what tales he whispered
    As he rode there by me,
Of friends whose smiling faces
    I am so soon to see.
And the mountains frowned in anger,
    Because I balked their spite,
And met my old-time comrade
    There on their very height;

But I laughed up in their faces,
    As I rode slowly back,
While the Wind went faster and faster,
    Like a race-horse on the track.

AT AN OLD DRAWER.

Before this scarf was faded,
　　What hours of mirth it knew;
How gayly it paraded
　　From smiling eyes to view.
The days were tinged with glory,
　　The nights too quickly sped,
And life was like a story
　　Where all the people wed.

Before this rosebud wilted,
　　How passionately sweet
The wild waltz swelled and lilted
　　In time for flying feet;
How loud the bassoons muttered,
　　The horns grew madly shrill,
And oh! the vows lips uttered
　　That hearts could not fulfill.

Before this fan was broken,
　　Behind its lace and pearl
What whispered words were spoken,
　　What hearts were in a whirl;

What homesteads were selected
　　In Fancy's realm of Spain,
What castles were erected
　　Without a room for pain.

When this odd glove was mated,
　　How thrilling seemed the play;
Maybe our hearts are sated—
　　We tire so soon to-day.
O, thrust away these treasures,
　　They speak the dreary truth;
We have outgrown the pleasures
　　And keen delights of youth.

SO LONG IN COMING.

When shall I hear the thrushes sing,
 And see their graceful, round throats swelling?
When shall I watch the bluebirds bring
 The straws and twiglets for their dwelling?
When shall I hear among the trees
 The little martial partridge drumming?
Oh! hasten! sights and sounds that please—
 The summer is so long in coming.

The winds are talking with the sun;
 I hope they will combine together
And melt the snow-drifts, one by one,
 And bring again the golden weather.
Oh haste, make haste, dear sun and wind,
 I long to hear the brown bee humming;
I seek for blooms I cannot find,
 The summer is so long coming.

The winter has been cold, so cold;
 Its winds are harsh, and bleak, and dreary,
And all its sports are stale and old;
 We wait for something now more cheery.

Come up, O summer, from the south,
   And bring the harps your hands are thrumming.
We pine for kisses from your mouth!
   Oh! do not be long in coming.

LAY IT AWAY.

We will lay our summer away, my friend,
　So tenderly lay it away.
It was bright and sweet to the very end,
　Like one long, golden day.
Nothing sweeter could come to me,
　Nothing sweeter to you.
We will lay it away, and let it be,
　Hid from the whole world's view.

We will lay it away like a dear, dead thing—
　Dead, yet forever fair;
And the fresh green robes of a deathless spring,
　Though dead, it shall always wear.
We will not hide it in grave or tomb,
　But lay it away to sleep,
Guarded by beauty, and light, and bloom,
　Wrapped in a slumber deep.

We were willing to let the summer go—
　Willing to go our ways;
But never on earth again I know
　Will either find such days.

You are my friend, and it may seem strange,
　　But I would not see you again;
I would think of you, though all things change,
　　Just as I knew you then.

If we should go back to the olden place,
　　And the summer time went, too,
It would be like looking a ghost in the face,
　　So much would be changed and new.
We cannot live it over again,
　　Not even a single day;
And as something sweet, and free from pain,
　　We had better lay it away.

PERISHED.

I called to the summer sun,
"Come over the hills to-day!
Unlock the rivers, and tell them to run,
And kiss the snow-drifts and melt them away."
And the sun came over—a tardy lover—
And unlocked the river, and told it to glide
And kissed the snow-drift till it fainted and died.

I called to the robin, "Come back!
Come up from the south and sing!"
And robin sailed up on an airy track.
And smoothed down his feathers and oiled his
wing.
And the notes came gushing, gurgling, rushing,
In thrills and quavers, clear, mellow and strong,
Till the glad air quivered and rang with song.

I said to the orchard, "Blow!"
I said to the meadow, "Bloom!"
And the trees stood white, like brides in a row,
And the breeze was laden with rare perfume.
And over the meadows, in lights and shadows,
The daisies white and violets blue,
And yellow-haired buttercups blossomed and
grew.

I called to a hope, that died
With the death of the flowers and grass,
  "Come back! for the river is free to glide—
The robin sings, and the daisies bloom." Alas!
  For the hope I cherished too rudely perished
  To ever awaken and live again,
  Though a hundred summers creep over the plain.

THE BELLE'S SOLILOQUY.

Heigh ho! well, the season's over!
  Once again we've come to Lent!
Programme's changed from balls and parties—
  Now we're ordered to repent.
Forty days of self-denial!
  Tell you what I think it pays—
Know 't'l freshen my complexion
  Going slow for forty days.

No more savory Frenchy suppers—
  Such as Madame R— can give.
Well, I need a little *thinning*—
  Just a trifle—sure's you live!
Sometimes been afraid my plumpness
  Might grow into downright fat.
Rector urges need of fasting—
  Think there's lot of truth in that.

We must meditate, he tells us,
  On our several acts of sin.
And repent them. Let me see now—
  Whereabouts shall I begin!

Flirting—yes, they say 'tis wicked;
  Well, I'm awful penitent.
(Wonder if my handsome major
  Goes to early Mass through Lent?)

Love of dress! I'm guilty there, too—
  Guess it's my besetting sin.
Still I'm somewhat like the lilies,
  For I neither toil nor spin.
Forty days I'll wear my plainest—
  Could repentance be more true?
What a saving on my dresses!
  They'll make over just like new.

Pride, and worldliness and all that,
  Rector bade us pray about
Every day through Lenten season,
  And I mean to be devout!
Papa always talks retrenchment—
  Lent is just the very thing.
Hope he'll get enough in pocket
  So we'll move up town next spring.

MY VISION.

Wherever my feet may wander
  Wherever I chance to be,
There comes, with the coming of even' time
  A vision sweet to me.
I see my mother sitting
  In the old familiar place,
And she rocks to the tune her needles sing,
  And thinks of an absent face.

I can hear the roar of the city
  About me now as I write;
But over an hundred miles of snow
  My thought-steeds fly to-night,
To the dear little cozy cottage,
  And the room where mother sits,
And slowly rocks in her easy chair
  And thinks of me as she knits.

Sometimes with the merry dancers
  When my feet are keeping time,
And my heart beats high, as young hearts will,
  To the music's rhythmic chime.

My spirit slips over the distance
　　Over the glitter and whirl,
To my mother who sits, and rocks, and knits,
　　And thinks of her "little girl."

When I listen to voices that flatter,
　　And smile, as women do,
To whispered words that may be sweet,
　　But are not always true;
I think of the sweet, quaint picture
　　Afar in quiet ways,
And I know one smile of my mother's eyes
　　Is better than all their praise.

And I know I can never wander
　　Far from the path of right,
Though snares are set for a woman's feet
　　In places that seem most bright.
For the vision is with me always,
　　Wherever I chance to be,
Of mother sitting, rocking and knitting,
　　Thinking and praying for me.

DREAM-TIME.

Throughout these mellow autumn days,
All sweet, and dim, and soft with haze,
I argue with my unwise heart,
That fain would choose the idler's part.

My heart says, "Let us lie and dream
Under the sunshine's softened beam,
This is the dream-time of the year,
When Heaven itself seems bending near.

"See how the calm waters lie
And dream beneath the arching sky.
The sun draws on a veil of haze,
And dreams away these golden days.

"Put by the pen—lay thought aside,
And cease to battle with the tide.
Let us, like Nature, rest and dream
And float with the current of the stream."

So pleads my heart. I answer "Nay,
Work waits for you and me to-day.
Behind these autumn hours of gold
The winter lingers, bleak and cold.

"And those who dream too long or much,
Must waken, shivering, at his touch,
With naught to show for vanished hours,
But dust of dreams and withered flowers.

"So now, while days are soft and warm,
We must make ready for the storm."
Thus, through this golden, hazy weather
My heart and I converse together.

And yet, I dare not turn my eyes
To pebbly shores or tender skies,
Because I am so fain to do,
E'en as my heart pleads with me to.

SING TO ME.

Sing to me! something of sunlight and bloom,
I am so compassed with sorrow and gloom,
I am so sick with the world's noise and strife,—
Sing of the beauty and brightness of life—
     Sing to me, sing to me!

Sing to me! something that's jubilant, glad!
I am so weary, my soul is so sad.
All my earth riches are covered with rust,
All my bright dreams are but ashes and dust.
     Sing to me, sing to me!

Sing of the blossoms that open in spring,
How the sweet flowers blow, and the long lichens
    cling,
Say, though the winter is round about me,
There are bright summers and springs yet to be.
    Sing to me, sing to me!

Sing me a song full of hope and of truth,
Brimming with all the sweet fancies of youth!

Say, though my sorrow I may not forget,
I have not quite done with happiness yet.
   Sing to me, sing to me!

Lay your soft fingers just here, on my cheek;
Turn the light lower—there—no, do not speak,
But sing! My heart thrills at your beautiful voice;
Sing till I turn from my grief and rejoice.
   Sing to me, sing to me!

SUMMER SONG.

The meadow lark's thrill and the brown thrush's
    whistle
From morning to evening fill all the sweet air,
And my heart is as light as the down of a thistle—
    The world is so bright and the earth is so fair.
There is life in the wood, there is bloom on the
    meadow;
    The air drips with songs that the merry birds
    sing.
The sunshine has won, in the battle with shadow,
    And she's dressed the glad earth with robes of
    the spring.

The bee leaves his hive for the field of red clover
    And the vale where the daisies bloom white as
    the snow,
And a mantle of warm yellow sunshine hangs over
    The calm little pond, where the pale lilies grow.
In the woodland beyond it, a thousand gay voices
    Are singing in chorus some jubilant air.
The bird and the bee, and all nature rejoices,
    The world is so bright, and the earth is so fair.

I am glad as a child, in this beautiful weather;
  I have tossed all my burdens and trials away;
My heart is as light—yes, as light as a feather;—
  I am care-free, and careless, and happy to-day.
Can it be there approaches a dark, drear to-
    morrow?
  Can shadows e'er fall on this beautiful earth?
Ah! to-day is my own! no forebodings of sorrow
  Shall darken my skies, or shall dampen my
    mirth.

A TWILIGHT THOUGHT.

The sweet maid, Day, has pillowed her head
　On the breast of her dusky lover, Night.
The sun has made her a couch of red,
　And wove her a mantle of soft twilight;
And the lover kisses the maiden's brow,
As low on her couch, she sleepeth now.

Here at my window, above the street,
　I sit as the day lies in repose;
And I list to the ceaseless tramp of feet,
　And I watch the human tide that flows
Upward and downward, and to and fro,
As the waves of an ocean ebb and flow.

Over and over the busy town;
　Hither and thither through all the day,
One goes up, and another down,
　Each in his own allotted way.
Strangers and kinsmen pass and meet,
And jar and jostle upon the street.

People that never met before,
　People that will not meet again;
A careless glance of the eye, no more,
　And both are lost in the sea of men.

Strangers divided by miles, in heart,
Under my window meet, and part.

But whether their feet walk up or down,
· Over the river, east or west;
Whether it's in, or out of the town,
    To a haunt of sin, or a home of rest,—
They are journeying to a common goal—
There is one *last* point for every soul!

Strangers and kinsmen, friend and foe,
    Whether their aims are great or small,
Whether their paths are high or low—
    There is one last resting-place for all.
They upward and onward, go surging by
Under my window—you all must die.

THE BELLE OF THE SEASON.

Nay—do not bring the jewels—
  Away with that robe of white,
I am sick of the ball room, sister—
  I would rather stay here, to-night.
"The grandest ball of the season!"
  "The upper-ten thousands' show!"
Yes, yes, I know it, my darling,
  But I do not care to go.

Last night I was thinking deeply,
  Something I seldom do.
You know I came home at midnight,
  Well, I lay awake till two.
I was thinking of my girlhood,
  Just how I had spent its years,
And I blushed for shame, my darling,
  And my pillow was wet with tears.

I have lived in a whirl of fashion,
  I have kept right up to the "style,"
I have learned how to dance the "German,"
  How to bow, and flirt and smile.

I have worn most beautiful dresses,
   Been the belle of many a ball.
I have won the envy of women,
   And the praise of fops—that's all.

Does any one really respect me?—
   Could a single thing be said
That would give the mourners pleasure
   To-morrow, if I were dead?
"She wore such beautiful dresses,"
   "She's a dozen strings to her bow,"
"She could waltz like a perfect fairy"-
   Would you like me remembered so?

Well, there's nothing else to remember—
   What thing have I ever done
That has made a soul the better
   Or cheered a hapless one?
I have spent my time and money—
   The best of my fortune and days—
In gaining the envy of women
   And making the poor fops gaze.

I am going to be a woman,
   And live for others awhile—
Forgetting myself for a season,
   Though I know it isn't the "style."

I am in no mood for a revel—
    Away with that robe of white!
And I will stay here, my darling,
    And talk with my heart to-night.

JOY. see p. 81

My heart is like a little bird
  That sits and sings for very gladness.
Sorrow is some forgotten word,
  And so, except in rhyme, is sadness.

The world is very fair to me—
  Such azure skies, such golden weather,
I'm like a long caged bird set free,
  My heart is lighter than a feather.

I rise rejoicing in my life;
  I live with love for God and neighbor;
My days flow on unmarred by strife,
  And sweetened by my pleasant labor.

Oh youth! oh spring! oh happy days,
  Ye are so passing sweet, and tender,
And while the fleeting season stays,
  I'll revel care-free, in its splendor.

*geep. 113
p. 80*

BIRD OF HOPE.

Soar not too high, oh bird of Hope!
  Because the skies are fair;
The tempest may come on apace
  And overcome thee there.

When far above the mountain tops
  Thou soarest, over all—
If, then, the storm should press thee back,
  How great would be thy fall!

And thou would'st lie here at my feet,
  A poor and lifeless thing,—
A torn and bleeding birdling,
  With a limp and broken wing.

Sing not too loud, oh bird of Hope!
  Because the day is bright;
The sunshine cannot always last—
  The morn precedes the night.

And if thy song is of the day,
  Then when the day grows dim,
Forlorn and voiceless thou wouldst sit
  Among the shadows grim.

Oh! I would have thee soar and sing,
    But not too high, or loud,
Remembering that day meets night—
    The brilliant sun the cloud.

A GOLDEN DAY.

The subtle beauty of this day
   Hangs o'er me like a fairy spell,
And care and grief have flown away,
   And every breeze sings, "All is well."
I ask, "Holds earth or sin, or woe?"
   My heart replies, "I do not know."

Nay! all we know, or feel, my heart,
   Today is joy undimmed, complete;
In tears or pain we have no part;
   The act of breathing is so sweet,
We care no higher joy to name.
   What reck we now of wealth or fame?

The past—what matters it to me?
   The pain it gave has passed away.
The future—that I cannot see!
   I care for nothing save today —
This is a respite from all care,
   And trouble flies—I know not where.

Go on, oh, noisy, restless life!
   Pass by, oh, feet that seek for heights!

POEMS OF REFLECTION.

I have no part in aught of strife;
   I do not want your vain delights.
The day wraps round me like a spell
   And every breeze sings, "All is well."

FADING.

All in the beautiful Autumn weather
  One thought lingers with me and stays;
Death and winter are coming together,
  Though both are veiled by the amber haze.
I look on the forest of royal splendor!
  I look on the face in my quiet room;
A face all beautiful, sad and tender,
  And both are stamped with the seal of doom.

All through the days of Indian summer,
  Minute by minute and hour by hour,
I feel the approach of a dreaded Comer—
  A ghastly presence of awful power.
I hear the birds in the early morning,
  As they fly from the fields that are turning
    brown,
And at noon and at night my heart takes warning,
  For the maple leaves fall down and down.

The sumac bushes are all a-flaming!
  The world is scarlet, and gold, and green,
And my darling's beautiful cheeks are shaming
  The painted bloom of the ballroom queen.

Why talk of winter, amid such glory?
  Why speak of death of a thing so fair?
Oh, but the forest king white and hoary
  Is weaving a mantle for both to wear.

God! if I could by the soft deceiving
  Of forests of splendor and cheeks of bloom
Lull my heart into sweet believing
  Just for a moment and drown my gloom;
If 1 could forget for a second only
  And rest from the pain of this awful dread
Of days that are coming long and lonely
  When the Autumn goes and she is dead.

But all the while the sun gilds wood and meadow
  And the fair cheeks, hectic glows and cheats,
I know grim death sits veiled in shadow
  Weaving for both their winding sheets.
I cannot help, and I cannot save her.
  My hands are as weak as a babe's, new-born;
I must yield her up to One who gave her
  And wait for the resurrection morn.

ALL THE WORLD.

see p. 12

*p. 12
p. 31*

*—see p. 12
p. 28*

This shining young

~~All the~~ world is full of babies,
  Sobbing, sighing everywhere,
Looking out with eyes of terror,
  Beating at the empty air.
Do they see the strife before them,
  That they sob and tremble so?
Oh, the helpless, frightened babies;
  Still they come and still they go.

Fresh, young

All ~~the~~ world is full of children,
  Laughing over little joys;
Sighing over little troubles—
  Fingers bruised or broken toys—
Wishing to be older, larger,
  Weeping at some fancied woe.
Oh, the happy, hapless, children,
  Still they come and still they go.

Amorous
Ardent

All ~~the~~ earth is full of lovers,
  Walking slowly, whispering sweet,
Dreaming dreams and building castles
  That must crumble at their feet;

Breaking vows and burning letters,
  Smiling lest the world shall know.
Oh, the foolish, trusting lovers,
  Still they come and still they go.

All the world is full of people,
  Hurrying, pushing, rushing by,
Bearing burdens, carrying crosses,
  Passing onward with a sigh;
Some like us, with smiling faces,
  And their heavy hearts below.
Oh, the sad-eyed, burdened people —
  How they come and how they go!

All the earth is full of corpses,
  Dust and bones, laid there to rest,
This the end, that babes and children,
  Lovers, people find at best;
All their cares and all their burdens,
  All their sorrows, wearing so—
Oh, the silent, happy corpses,
  Sleeping soundly, lying low.

LINES.

Dedicated to Mr. and Mrs. D. Atwood upon the celebration of their silver wedding, August 25th, 1874.

The harvest-moon of wedded love,
  Fair in the heavens sailing,
Has reached mid-height, and, clear and bright,
  Gives little sign of paling.

Since first, above the horizon,
  The silvery crescent lifted,
The clouds of five-and-twenty years
  Have o'er its surface drifted.

But, while the days have come and gone,
  Though many a changing "morrow,"
The growing moon sailed up and on
  Above the hills of sorrow.

And, though with years came blinding tears,
  The guiding moon grew brighter;
It gave relief, in time of grief—
  Made heavy burdens lighter.

One quarter of one hundred years
   It has been growing, filling,
Till, round and bright, its silvery light
   On all tonight is spilling.

Oh, harvesters on life's great plain!
   The young sheaves shining 'round you
Prove that you have not toiled in vain—
   Prove that God's blessing found you.

Smile in the moonlight's silver gleam,
   Rejoice in harvest weather;
Ye know ye may not always keep
   The precious sheaves together!

Shine on, oh moon of wedded bliss!
   Live on through many a morrow,
Till from the sun of Immortal Love
   Its golden light you borrow.

A FRAGMENT.

Your words came just when needed. Like a breeze,
Blowing and bringing from the wide salt sea
Some cooling spray, to meadow scorched with heat
And choked with dust and clouds of sifted sand,
That hateful whirlwinds, envious of its bloom,
Had tossed upon it. But the cool sea breeze
Came laden with the odors of the sea
And damp with spray, that laid the dust and sand
And brought new life and strength to blade and
    bloom,
So words of thine came over miles to me,
Fresh from the mighty sea, a true friend's heart,
And brought me hope, and strength, and swept
    away
The dusty webs that human spiders spun
Across my path. Friend—and the word means
    much—
So few there are who reach like thee, a hand
Up over all the barking curs of spite
And give the clasp, when most its need is felt;
Friend, newly found, accept my full heart's thanks.

THE CHANGE.

She leaned out into the soft June weather,
　　With her long loose tresses the night breeze
　　　　played;
Her eyes were as blue as the bells on the heather:
　　Oh, what is so fair as a fair young maid!

She folded her hands, like the leaves of a lily,
　　"My life," she said, "is a night in June,
Fair and quiet, and calm and stilly;
　　Bring me a change, oh changeful moon!

"Who would drift on a lake forever?
　　Young hearts weary—it is not strange,
And sigh for the beautiful bounding river;
　　New moon, true moon, bring me a change!"

The rose that rivaled her maiden blushes
　　Dropped from her breast, at a stranger's feet;
Only a glance; but the hot blood rushes
　　To mantle a fair face, shy and sweet.

To and fro, while the moon is waning,
　They walk, and the stars shine on above;
And one is in earnest, and one is feigning—
　Oh, what is so sweet, as a sweet young love?

A young life crushed, and a young heart broken,
　A bleak wind blows through the lovely bower,
And all that remains of the love vows spoken—
　Is the trampled leaf of a faded flower.

The night is dark, for the moon is failing—
　And what is so pale, as a pale old moon!
Cold is the wind through the tree tops wailing—
　Woe that the change should come so soon.

OLD.

They stood together at the garden gate;
They heard the night bird calling to his mate;
    The sun had set,
And all the vines upon the summer bowers,
The long green grasses, and the blooming flowers
    Were dewy wet.

The sun's last rays had lit the Western skies
And dipped the mass of clouds in golden dyes
    Brilliant and grand.
They stood in silence for a little while,
And then he turned, and with a tender smile
    He took her hand.

"Of all the sweet days we have known, my friend,"
He said half sadly, "This will be the end.
    I grieve to go,
Loving, as I shall never love again;
It rends my heart-strings, and it gives me pain,
    But well I know

"I could not make you happy with my love,
You, tender hearted, gentle as a dove,

And I—oh, well!
I cannot grovel on in this dull life.
How my soul yearns for scenes of noise and strife
No tongue can tell.

And so I give you back the pledge you gave,
I should but drag you to an early grave
With my unrest.
You are unfettered; but here at your feet
I leave my heart; oh, may you be, my sweet,
Forever blest.''

She drew from off her hand the hoop of gold
(Dearer to her by far than wealth untold)
And gave to him,
And as she, slow and silent, moved away,
Her life like all that Western sky grew gray
And bleak and grim.

He walks to-day, with kings upon the earth;
He dwells in scenes of revelry and mirth,
With naught of care.
And she—the sun that set for her in deepest gloom,
And never rose, will rise beyond the tomb
And meet her there.

THE MUSICIANS.

The strings of my heart were strung by Pleasure,
    And I laughed when the music fell on my ear,
For he and Mirth played a joyful measure,
    And they played so loud that I could not hear
The wailing and mourning of souls a-weary—
    The strains of sorrow that floated around,
For my heart's notes rang out loud and cheery,
    And I heard no other sound.

Mirth and Pleasure, the music brothers,
    Played louder and louder in joyful glee;
But sometimes a discord was heard by others—
    Though only the rhythm was heard by me.
Louder and louder, and faster and faster
    The hands of the brothers played strain on strain,
When all of a sudden a Mighty Master
    Swept them aside; and Pain,

Pain, the musician, the soul-refiner,
    Restrung the strings of my quivering heart,
And the air that he played was a plaintiff minor,
    So sad that the tear-drops were forced to start;

Each note was an echo of awful anguish,
　　As shrill as solemn, as sharp as slow,
And my soul for a season, seemed to languish
　　And faint with its weight of woe.

With skilful hands that were never weary,
　　This Master of Music played strain on strain,
And between the bars of the miserere,
　　He drew up the strings of my heart again,
And I was filled with a vague, strange wonder,
　　To see that they did not snap in two.
"They　are　drawn　so　tight,　they　will　break
　　　　asunder,"
　　I thought, but instead, they grew.

In the hands of the Master, firmer and stronger;
　　And I could hear on the stilly air—
Now my ears were deafened by Mirth no longer—
　　The sound of sorrow, and grief, and despair;
And my soul grew kinder and tender to others,
　　My nature grew sweeter, my mind grew broad,
And I held all men to be my brothers,
　　Linked by the chastening rod.

My soul was lifted to God and heaven,
　　And when on my heart-strings fell again
The hands of Mirth, and Pleasure, even,
　　There was never a discord to mar the strain.

For Pain, the musician, and soul-refiner,
  Attuned the strings with a master hand,
And whether the music be major or minor,
  It is always sweet and grand.

THE DOOMED CITY'S PRAYER.

I heard a low sound, like a troubled soul praying:
   And the winds of a winter night brought it to me.
'Twas the doomed city's voice: "Oh, kind snow,"
      it was saying,
   "Come cover my ruins, so ghastly to see.
I am robbed of my beauty, and shorn of my glory;
   And the strength that I boasted—where is it to-
      day?
I am down in the dust; and my pitiful story
   Makes tearless eyes weep and unpious lips pray.

"I—I, who have reveled in pomp and in power,
   Am down on my knees, with my face in the dust;
But yesterday queen, with a queen's royal dower,
   To-day I am glad of a crumb or a crust.
But yesterday reigning, a grand, mighty city,
   The pride of the Nation, and queen of the West;
To-day I am gazed at, an object of pity,
   A charity child, asking alms, at the best.

"My strength, and my pride, and my glory de-
     parted,
   My fair features scorched by the fire fiend's
     breath,

Is it strange that I'm soul-sick, and sorrowful
  hearted?
  Is it strange that my thoughts run on ruin and
    death?
Oh, white, fleecy clouds that are drooping above me,
  Hark, hark to my pleadings, and answer my
    sighs,
And let down the beautiful snow, if you love me,
  To cover my wounds from all pitying eyes.

.

"'I am hurled from my throne, but not hurled down
  forever;
  I shall rise from the dust, I shall live down my
    woes—
But my heart lies, to-day, like a dumb, frozen
  river;
  When to thaw out and flow again, God only
    knows.
Oh, sprites of the air! I beseech you to weave me
  A mantle of white snow, and beautiful rime
To cover my unsightly ruins; then leave me
  In the hands of the healer of all wounds—'Old
    Time.'"

DAFT.

In the warm yellow smile of the morning,
   She stands at the lattice pane,
And watches the strong young binders
   Stride down to the fields of grain,
And she counts them over and over
   As they pass her cottage door:
Are they six, she counts them seven—
   Are they seven, she counts one more.

When the sun swings high in the heavens,
   And the reapers go shouting home,
She calls to the household, saying,
   "Make haste! for the binders have come!
And Johnnie will want his dinner—
   He was always a hungry child;"
And they answer, "Yes, it is waiting;"
   Then tell you, "Her brain is wild."

Again, in the hush of the evening,
   When the work of the day is done,
And the binders go singing homeward
   In the last red rays of the sun,

She will sit at the threshold waiting,
　And her withered face lights with joy:
"Come, Johnnie," she says, as they pass her,
　"Come into the house, my boy."

Five summers ago her Johnnie
　Went out in the smile of the morn,
Singing across the meadow,
　Striding down through the corn—
He towered above the binders,
　Walking on either side,
And the mother's heart within her
　Swelled with exultant pride.

For he was the light of the household—
　His brown eyes were wells of truth,
And his face was the face of the morning,
　Lit with its pure, fresh youth,
And his song rang out from the hilltops
　Like the mellow blast of a horn,
And he strode o'er the fresh shorn meadows,
　And down through the rows of corn.

But hushed were the voices of singing,
　Hushed by the presence of death,
As back to the cottage they bore him—
　In the noontide's scorching breath,

For the heat of the sun had slain him,
  Had smitten the heart in his breast,
And he who had towered above them
  Lay lower than all the rest.

The grain grows ripe in the sunshine,
  And the summers ebb and flow,
And the binders stride to their labor
  And sing as they come and go;
But never again from the hilltops
  Echoes the voice like a horn;
Never up from the meadows,
  Never back from the corn.

Yet the poor, crazed brain of the mother
  Fancies him always near;
She is blest in her strange delusion,
  For she knoweth no pain nor fear,
And always she counts the binders
  As they pass her cottage door;
Are they six, she counts them seven;
  Are they seven, she counts them more.

HUNG.

Nine o'clock, and the sun shines as yellow and
      warm
As though 'twere a fete day. I wish it would
      storm :
    Wish the thunder would crash,
    And the red lightning flash,
And lap the black clouds with its serpentine tongue.
The day is too calm for a man to be hung.
    Hung! Ugh, what a word!
The most heartless and horrible ear ever heard.

He has murdered, and plundered, and robbed, so
      "they say";
Been a scourge of the country for many a day.
    He was lawless and wild;
    Man, woman or child
Met no mercy, no pity, if found in his path;
He was worse than a beast of the woods, in his
      wrath.
    And yet—to be hung,
    Oh, my God! to be swung
By the neck to and fro for the rabble to see—
    The thought sickens me.

Thirty minutes past nine. How the time hurries by,
But the half hour remains—at ten he will die.
    Die? No! He'll be killed!
    For God never willed
    Men should die in this way.
"Vengeance is mine," He saith. "I will repay."
    Yet what could be done
    With this wild, lawless one!
No prison could hold him, and so—he must swing.
    It's a horrible thing!

Outcast, desperado, fiend, knave; all of these
And more. But call him whatever you please,
    I cannot forget
    He's a mortal man yet:
That he once was a babe and was hushed into rest,
And fondled and pressed to a woman's warm
      breast.
    Was sung to and rocked,
    And when he first walked
With his weak little feet, he was petted and told
He was "mamma's own pet, worth his whole weight
      in gold."
    And this is the end
Of a God-given life. Just think of it, friend!

Hark! hear you that chime? 'Tis the clock strik-
      ing ten.
The dread weight falls down, with a sound like
      "Amen."

Does murder pay murder? Do two wrongs make a
      right?
    Oh, that horrible sight!
I am shut in my room and have covered my face,
But the dread scene has followed me into this place.
      I see that strange thing,
      Like a clock pendulum, swing
To and fro, in the air, back and forth, to and fro.
      One moment ago
'Twas a man in God's image. Now hide it, kind
      grave.
Oh, God, what an end to the life that you gave!

WHEN I AM DEAD.

When I am dead, if some chastened one,
   Seeing the "item," or hearing it said
That my play is over and my part done,
   And I lie asleep in my narrow bed—
If I could know that some soul would say,
   Speaking aloud or silently,
"In the heat and the burden of the day
   She gave a refreshing draught to me;"

Or, "When I was lying nigh unto death
   She nursed me to life and to strength again,
And when I labored and struggled for breath
   She smoothed and quieted down my pain;"
Or, "When I was groping in grief and doubt,
   Lost, and turned from the light o' the day,
Her hand reached me and helped me out
   And led me up to the better way;"

Or, "When I was hated and shunned by all,
   Bowing under my sin and my shame,
She, once in passing me by, let fall
   Words of pity and hope, that came

Into my heart like a blessed calm
    Over the waves of the stormy sea,
Words of comfort, like oil and balm,
    She spake, and the desert blossomed for me;"

Better, by far, than a marble tomb—
    Than a monument towering over my head
(What shall I care, in my quiet room,
    For headboard or footboard when I am dead?);
Better than glory, or honors, or fame
    (Though I am striving for those to-day),
To know that some heart would cherish my name
    And think of me kindly, with blessings, alway.

IN MEMORY OF MISS JENNY BLANCHARD.

Across the sodden fields we gaze,
  To woodlands, painted gold and brown;
To hills that hide in purple haze
  And proudly wear the Autumn's crown.
Oh, lavish Autumn! fair, we know,
  And yet we cannot deem her so.

The blossoms had their day;
  To grasses and to green-hung trees.
They lived, grew old and passed away.
  And yet, not satisfied with these,
The cruel Autumn will not pass
  Without this keen, fell stroke.   Alas!

"Alas!" we cry, because God's ways
  Seem so at variance with our own,
And, grieving through the nights and days,
  We see not that His love was shown
In gathering to His "Harvest Home"
  Our lost one, from the grief to come.

Oh, tears! she will not have to weep!
  Oh, woes! she will not have to bear!
For her, who fell so soon asleep,
  No furrowed face, no whitened hair.
And yet we would have given her these
  In lieu of heavenly victories.

How weak the strongest mortal love!
  How selfish in its tenderness!
How God's angelic host above
  Must wonder at our blind distress!
We see her still grave, dark and dim,
  And they see only Heaven and Him.

Perpetual youth! Oh, priceless boon!
  Forever youthful, never old!
How can we think she died too soon?
  What though life's story was half told?
Wiser than all earth seers, to-day,
  Is this fair soul that passed away.

Magician, sage, philosopher,
  With all their vast brain-wealth combined,
Are only babes compared with her:
  This soul that left the "things behind"
And, "reaching to the things before,"
  Gained God, through Christ, forevermore.

IN MEMORY OF J. B.

Brave heart, whose bed has now been made
  A twelve month neath the grasses,
Checkered by sunshine and by shade,
  Where every breeze that passes
Hushes its song and sighs along,
  With sorrow in its cadence,
Not thinking how thy sainted brow
  Glows with a Christly radiance.

Do spirits hover in the air?
  Do the dear dead ones never
Float on the gentle zyphers near
  Out of the vast forever?
Somehow to-day my thoughts will stray
  To you, oh friend, in slumber!
You seem so near, I feel you here,
  One of the angel number.

Oh, face I never looked upon!
  Oh, quiet, dreamless sleeper!.
How strange that when you journeyed on
  With death, the mighty reaper,

I missed you so. Do angels know,
   Up in the City's splendor,
When hearts on earth embalm their worth,
   And are they glad, I wonder?

BIRD OF HOPE. see p. 81

Oh, Bird of Hope! soar not too high
  Because the skies are fair;
The tempest may come on apace
  And overcome thee there.

When high above the mountain tops
  Thou soarest over all,
If then the storm should press thee back
  How great would be thy fall!

And thou wouldst lie here at my feet,
  A poor and lifeless thing—
A torn and bleeding birdling, with
  A limp and broken wing.

Sing not too loud, oh, bird of hope!
  Because the day is bright;
The sunshine cannot always last—
  The morn precedes the night.

And if thy song is of the day,
  Then, when the day grows dim,
Forlorn and voiceless, thou wilt sit
  Among the shadows grim.

Oh! I would have thee soar and sing,
But not too high and loud:
Remembering that day meets night—
The brilliant sun the cloud.

GHOSTS.

There are ghosts in the room,
As I sit here alone, from the dark corners there
    They come out of the gloom
And they stand at my side and they lean on my
        chair.

There's the ghost of a Hope
That lighted my days with a fanciful glow;
    In her hand is the rope
That strangled her life out. Hope was slain long
        ago.

But her ghost comes to-night,
With its skeleton face and expressionless eyes,
    And it stands in the light
And mocks me and jeers me with sobs and with
        sighs.

There's a ghost of a Joy,
A frail, fragile thing, and I prized it too much,
    And the hands that destroy
Clasped it close, and it died at the withering touch.

There's a ghost of a Love,
Born with Joy, reared with Hope, died in pain and
      unrest;
   But he towers above
All the others—this ghost: yet a ghost at the best.

   I am weary, and fain
Would forget all these dead; but the gibbering host
   Make my struggle in vain.
In each shadowy corner there lurketh a ghost.

OUT OF THE DEPTHS.

Out of the midnight, rayless and starless,
  Into the morning's golden light;
Out of the clutches of wrong and ruin,
  Into the arms of truth and right;
Out of the ways that are ways of sorrow;
  Out of the paths that are paths of pain—
Yea! out of the depths has a soul arisen,
  And "one that is lost is found again!"

Lost in the sands of an awful desert!
  Lost in a region of imps accursed,
With bones of a victim to mark his pathway,
  And burning lava to quench his thirst.
Lost in the darkness, astray in the shadows—
  Father above, do we pray in vain?
Hark! on the winds come gleeful tidings:
  Lo, "he that was lost is found again."

Found! and the sunlight of God's great mercy
  Dispels the shadows and brings the morn;
Found! and the hosts of the dear Redeemer
  Are shouting aloud o'er a soul re-born.

Plucked, like a brand from the conflagration;
   Cleansed, like a garment free from stain;
Saved—pray God—for now and forever—
   Lost for a season, but found again.

"Out of the depths," by the grace of heaven,
   Out of the depths of woe and shame.
And he strikes his name from the roll of drunkards,
   To carve it again on the heights of fame,
"Wine is a mocker, strong drink is raging"—
   Glory to God, he has snapped the chain
That bound him with fetters of steel and iron;
   And "he that was lost is found again."

Down with the cup, though it gleams like rubies!
   Down with the glass, though it sparkle and shine!
"It bites like a serpent, and stings like an adder"—
   There is shame, and sorrow, and woe in wine.
Keen though the sword be, and deadly its mission,
   Three times its number the wine cup has slain.
God, send thy grace upon these it has fettered;
   God grant the lost may be found again.

MISTAKES.

My life is full of sad mistakes,—
　　Today I was thinking about them,
And thinking of all that I might have been
　　If I had but lived without them.
So many times have I laid my plan,
　　Only to spoil it in doing;
And much of the work that the world calls good
　　Has left me cause for rueing.

Each thing that I do is like the page
　　Of a hurriedly written letter;—
Full of good thoughts perhaps, but the blots
　　Prove that it might be better.
I have wished for the world's applause, and thought
　　To make it praise and wonder,
But my noblest aim and best laid plan
　　Was sure to be spoiled by a blunder.

I think I have lived too far from God,—
　　Not that I ever doubt Him,
But feeling too sure of my strength, I've tried
　　To do some things without Him.

And so we shall always make mistakes,
  And always our errors be rueing,
Until we reach up for the Guiding Hand,
  Whatever we may be doing.

PRESUMPTION.

Whenever I am prone to doubt or wonder—
  I check myself, and say, ''That mighty One
Who made the solar system cannot blunder—
  And for the best all things are being done.''
Who set the stars on their eternal courses
  Has fashioned this strange earth by some sure
    plan.
Bow low, bow low to those majestic forces
  Nor dare to doubt their wisdom—puny man.

You cannot put one little star in motion,
  You cannot shape one single forest leaf,
Nor fling a mountain up, nor sink an ocean,
  Presumptuous pigmy, large with unbelief.
You cannot bring one dawn of regal splendor
  Nor bid the day to shadowy twilight fall,
Nor send the pale moon forth with radiance tender,
  And dare you doubt the One who has done all?

''So much is wrong, there is such pain—such sin-
    ning.''
  Yet look again—behold how much is right!
And He who formed the world from its beginning
  Knows how to guide it upward to the light.

Your task, O man, is not to carp and cavil
   At God's achievements, but with purpose strong
To cling to good, and turn away from evil—
   That is the way to help the world along.

TWILIGHT THOUGHTS.

The God of the day has vanished,
  The light from the hills has fled,
And the hand of an unseen artist,
  Is painting the west all red.
All threaded with gold and crimson,
  And burnished with amber dye,
And tipped with purple shadows,
  The glory flameth high.

Fair, beautiful world of ours!
  Fair, beautiful world, but oh,
How darkened by pain and sorrow,
  How blackened by sin and woe.
The splendor pales in the heavens
  And dies in a golden gleam,
And alone in the hush of twilight,
  I sit, in a checkered dream.

I think of the souls that are straying,
  In shadows as black as night,
Of hands that are groping blindly
  In search of a shining light;

Of hearts that are mutely crying.
　And praying for just one ray,
To lead them out of the shadows,
　Into the better way.

And I think of the Father's children
　Who are trying to walk alone,
Who have dropped the hand of the Parent,
　And wander in ways unknown.
Oh, the paths are rough and thorny,
　And I know they cannot stand.
They will faint and fall by the wayside,
　Unguarded by God's right hand.

And I think of the souls that are yearning
　To follow the good and true;
They are striving to live unsullied,
　Yet I know not what to do.
And I wonder when God, the Master,
　Shall end this weary strife,
And lead us out of the shadows
　Into the deathless life.

LISTEN!

Whoever you are as you read this,
  Whatever your trouble or grief,
I want you to know and to heed this:
  The day draweth near with relief.

No sorrow, no woe is unending,
  Though heaven seems voiceless and dumb;
So sure as your cry is ascending,
  So surely an answer will come.

Whatever temptation is near you,
  Whose eyes on this simple verse fall;
Remember good angels will hear you
  And help you to stand, if you call.

Though stunned with despair I beseech you,
  Whatever your losses, your need,
Believe, when these printed words reach you
  Believe you were born to succeed.

You are stronger, I tell you, this minute,
　　Than any unfortunate fate!
And the coveted prize—you can win it;
　　While life lasts 'tis never too late!

SONG OF THE SPIRIT.

Too sweet and too subtle for pen or for tongue
In phrases unwritten and measures unsung,
As deep and as strange as the sounds of the sea,
Is the song that my spirit is singing to me.

In the midnight and tempest when forest trees
    shiver,
In the roar of the surf, and the rush of the river,
In the rustle of leaves and the fall of the rain,
And on the low breezes I catch the refrain.

From the vapors that frame and envelope the earth,
And beyond, from the realms where my spirit had
    birth,
From the mists of the land and the fogs of the sea,
Forever and ever the song comes to me.

I know not its wording—its import I know—
For the rythm is broken, the measure runs low,
When vexed or allured by the things of this life
My soul is merged into its pleasures or strife.

When up to the hill tops of beauty and light
My soul like a lark in the ether takes flight,
And the white gates of heaven shine brighter and
    nearer,
The song of the spirit grows sweeter and clearer.

Up, up to the realms where no mortal has trod—
Into space and infinity near to my God—
With whiteness, and silence, and beautiful things,
I am borne when the voice of eternity sings.

When once in the winds or the drop of the rain
Thy spirit shall listen and hear the refrain,
Thy soul shall soar up like a bird on the breeze,
And the things that have pleased thee will never
    more please.

THE PILGRIM FATHERS.

And now when poets are singing
  Their song of olden days,
And now, when the land is ringing
  With sweet Centennial lays,
My muse goes wandering backward
  To the groundwork of all these,
To the time when our Pilgrim Fathers
  Came over the winter seas.

The sons of a mighty kingdom,
  Of a cultured folk were they,
Born amidst pomp and splendor,
  Bred in it, day by day.   .
Children of bloom and beauty,
  Reared under skies serene,
Where the daisy and hawthorne blossomed
  And the ivy was always green.

And yet, for the sake of freedom,
  For a free religious faith,
They turned from home and people,
  And stood face to face with death.
They turned from a tyrant ruler
  And stood on the new world's shore,
With a waste of waters behind them,
  And a waste of land before.

Oh, men of a great Republic;
  Of a land of untold worth;
Of a nation that has no equal
  Upon God's round green earth;
I hear you sighing and crying
  Of the hard, close times at hand;
What think you of those old heroes,
  On the rock 'twixt sea and land.

The bells of a million churches
  Go ringing out to-night,
And the glitter of palace windows
  Fills all the land with light;
And there is the home and college,
  And here is the feast and ball,
And the angels of peace and freedom
  Are hovering over all.

They had no church, no college,
  No banks, no mining stock;
They had but the waste before them,
  The sea and Plymouth Rock.
But there in the night and tempest,
  With gloom on every hand,
They laid the first foundation
  Of a nation great and grand.

There were no weak repinings,
  No shrinking from what might be,
But with their brows to the tempest,
  And with their backs to the sea,

They planned out a noble future,
  And planted the corner-stone
Of the grandest, greatest republic
  The world has ever known.

Oh, women in homes of splendor,
  Oh lily-buds frail and fair,
With fortunes upon your fingers,
  And milk-white pearls in your hair,
I hear you longing and sighing
  For some new fresh delight;
But what of those Pilgrim mothers
  On that December night?

I hear you talking of hardships,
  I hear you moaning of loss,
Each has her fancied sorrow,
  Each bears her self-made cross.
But they, they had only their husbands,
  The rain, the rock, and the sea;
Yet, they looked up to God and blessed Him,
  And were glad because they were free.

Oh, grand old Pilgrim heroes,
  Oh, souls that were tried and true,
With all of our proud possessions
  We are humbled at thought of you.
Men of such might and muscle,
  Women so brave and strong,
Whose faith was fixed as the mountains,
  Through a night so dark and long.

We know of your grim, grave errors,
  As husbands and as wives;
Of the rigid bleak ideas
  That starved your daily lives;
Of pent-up, curbed emotions,
  Of feelings crushed, suppressed,
That God with the heart created
  In every human breast.

We know of the little remnant
  Of British tyranny,
When you hunted Quakers and witches,
  And swung them from a tree;
Yet back to a holy motive,
  To live in the fear of God,
To a purpose light, exalted,
  To walk where martyrs trod.

We can trace your gravest errors.
  Your aim was fixed and sure;
And e'en if your acts were fanatic,
  We know your hearts were pure.
You lived so near to heaven,
  You overreached your trust,
And deemed yourselves creators,
  Forgetting you were but dust.

But we with our broader visions,
  With our wider realms of thought,
I often think would be better
  If we lived as our fathers taught.

Their lives seemed bleak and rigid,
   Narrow and void of bloom;
Our minds have too much freedom,
   And conscience too much room.

They overreached in duty,
   They starved their hearts for the right;
We live too much in the senses,
   We bask too long in the light.
They proved by their clinging to Him
   The image of God in man;
And we, by our love of license,
   Strengthen a Darwin's plan.

But bigotry reached its limit,
   And license must have its sway,
And both shall result in profit
   To those of a later day.
With the fetters of slavery broken,
   And freedom's flag unfurled,
Our nation strides onward and upward,
   And stands the peer of the world.

Spires and domes and steeples
   Glitter from shore to shore;
The waters are white with commerce,
   The earth is studded with ore;
Peace is sitting above us,
   And Plenty, with laden hand,
Wedded to sturdy Labor,
   Goes singing through the land.

Then let each child of the nation
  Who glories in being free,
Remember the Pilgrim Fathers
  Who stood on the rock by the sea;
For there in the rain and tempest
  Of a night long passed away,
They sowed the seeds of a harvest
  We gather in sheaves to-day.

LINES WRITTEN UPON THE DEATH OF JAMES BUELL.

Something is missing from the balmy spring;
    There is no perfume in its gentle breath;
And there are sobs, in songs the wild birds sing,
    And all the bees chant of the grave and death—
Something is missing from the earth. One morn
    The angels called a new name on the roll;
A spirit-soldier to their ranks was borne,
    And all Christ's army welcomed the pure young
        soul.

He died. Two little words, but only God
    Can understand the awful depths of woe
They hold for those who pass beneath the rod,
    Praying for strength, from Him who aimed the
        blow.
He died. The soldier who fought long and well,
    Who walked with Death upon the battle-field,
Among the bellowing guns—the shrieking shell—
    In poison prison dens—and would not yield.

A six months three times told he languished there,
    And yet he lived; oh, young heart, strong and
        brave!

Thank God, who heard the oft repeated prayer;
  Thank God, he does not fill a Southern grave;
That when he died, the loved ones gathered round
  And eased the anguish of those last, sad hours;
That gentle hands can keep the precious mound
  All green with mosses, and abloom with flowers.

He was so young and fair; and life so sweet.
  Christ gives the mourners strength to drain the
      cup.
He went to make the Heavenly ranks complete.
  God sent the angel Death to bear him up
So young, and fair and brave; so loved by all;
  The lisping child-life's veteran, bent and gray—
The eyes grew dim, and bitter tear-drops fall
  Upon the mound where lies the soldier's clay.

Oh! it is sweet to feel that God knows best,
  Who called in youth this brother, friend, and son.
And sweet to lean upon the Saviour's breast,
  And looking upwards, say, "Thy will be done."
But something is missing from the balmy spring
  There is no perfume in its gentle breath,
And there are sobs in songs the wild birds sing,
  And all the bees chant of the grave and death.

SEARCHING.

These quiet autumn days,
My soul, like Noah's dove, on airy wings
Goes out and searches for the hidden things
　Beyond the hills of haze.

With mournful, pleading cries,
Above the waters of the voiceless sea
That laps the shores of Eternity,
　Day after day it flies.

Searching, but all in vain,
For some stray leaf that it may light upon
And read the future as the days agone—
　Its joy, its pain.

Listening, patiently,
For some voice speaking from the mighty deep,
Revealing all the things that it doth keep
　In secret there for me.

Come back and wait, my soul!
Day after day thy search has been in vain.
Voiceless and silent, o'er the future's pain,
　Its mistic waters roll.

God, seeing, knoweth best,
And day by day the waters shall subside,
And thou shalt know what lies beneath the tide;
Then wait, my soul, and rest.

FADING.

She sits beside the window. All who pass
   Turn once again to gaze on her sweet face.
She is so fair; but soon, too soon, alas,
   To lie down in her last resting-place.

No gems are brighter than her sparkling eyes,
   Her brow like polished marble, white and fair—
Her cheeks are glowing as the sunset skies—
   You would not dream that Death was lurking
      there.

But, oh! he lingers closely at her side,
   And when the forest dons her Autumn dress.
We know that he will claim her as his bride,
   And earth will number one fair spirit less.

She sees the meadow robed in richest green—
   The laughing stream—the willows bending o'er.
With tear dimmed eyes she views each sylvan scene,
   And thinks earth never was so fair before.

We do not sigh for heaven, till we have known,
  Something of sorrow, something of grief and
    woe,
And as a summer day her life has flown.
  Oh, can we wonder she is loth to go?

She has no friends in Heaven: all are here.
  No lost one waits her in that unknown land,
And life grows doubly, trebly sweet and dear
  As day by day she nears the mystic strand.

We love her and we grieve to see her go.
  But it is Christ who calls her to His breast,
And He shall greet her, and she soon shall know
  The joys of souls that dwell among the blest.

A DREAM.

The shadows of a winter night were falling,
  The snows were drifting in my cottage door—
And loud the voices of the winds were calling,
  When there came a stranger, lone, despised, and
    poor!

Came to my glowing hearth, all humbly pleading
  For food and shelter till the day should dawn—
But to his every word I stood unheeding,
  And turned him forth and bade him wander on.

I have six little ones to guard from danger;
  I have a pillow for each precious head;
But nought to waste upon a beggared stranger—
  And "charity begins at home," I said.

All fierce and loud the winter wind was groaning,
  Like some lost spirit, doomed to death it seemed;
While at some door it made its ceaseless moaning,
  I sought my pillow, and I slept and dreamed.

I dreamed I stood at Heaven's gate entreating,
  Weeping and wailing for the other side;
While in the gloom I stood, all wildly beating,
  Begging the angel guard to open wide.

At length I heard the pearly hinges turning,
   And saw the glories that no tongue can tell.
Before me all the hues of Heaven burning,
   Behind me all the gloom of death and hell.

I strove to enter, but a voice like thunder,
   Cried "Come no nearer, oh! thou soul of sin."
And I shrank down in awful fear and wonder,
   For I had thought to enter boldly in.

Again the voice cried, "When in woe and anguis.
   I sought a shelter at thy glowing hearth,
Thou turned me out, unclothed, unfed to languis.
   And wander wearily upon the earth.

"Depart from here, thou selfish sinful mortal,
   On heaven's perfect face, a stain and blot;
For never can'st thou cross the shining portal,
   Ye knew not me and now I know ye not."

IDLER'S SONG.

I sit in the twilight dim.
  At the close of an idle day,
And I list to the soft, sweet **hymn,**
  That rises far away,
And dies on the evening air.
  Oh, all day long,
  They sing their song,
Who toil in the valley there.

But never a song sing **I,**
  Sitting with folded hands,
The hours pass me by—
  Dropping their golden sands—
And I list, from day to day,
  To the "tick, tick, tock"
  Of the old brown clock,
Ticking my life away.

And I see the twilight fade,
  And I see the night come on,
And then, in the gloom and shade,
  I weep for the day that's gone—

Weep and wail in pain,
　For the misspent day
　That has flown away,
And will not come again.

Another morning beams,
　And I forget the last,
And I sit in idle dreams
　'Till the day is over—past.
Oh, the toiler's heart is glad!
　When the day is gone
　And the night comes on,
But mine is sore and sad.

For I dare not look behind!
　No shining, golden sheaves
Can I ever hope to find:
　Nothing but withered leaves,
Ah, dreams are very sweet!
　But will not please
　If only these
I lay at the Master's feet.

And what will the Master say
　To dreams and nothing more?
Oh, idler, all the day!
　Think, ere thy life is o'er!

And when the day grows late,
  Oh, soul of sin!
Will He let you in,
There at the pearly gate?

Oh, idle heart, beware!
  On, to the field of strife!
On, to the valley there!
  And live a useful life!
Up, do not wait a day!
  For the old brown clock,
  With its "tick, tick, tock"
Is ticking your life away.

FOR HIM WHO BEST SHALL UNDE STAND IT.

I know a "righteous Christian,"
  (That is, he thinks he's one,)
He goes to church on Sunday
  And thinks his duty done.
And always at prayer-meeting,
  He sighs, and groans, and prays;
And talks about the sinners,
  And warns them from their ways.

And many of his neighbors,
  He knows are bound for hell;
Although they love their Master,
  And do their duty well.
But they pray within their closet,
  And do not own a "pew,"
And he's sure they'll not be numbered
  Among God's chosen few.

He exhorts men to be careful
  And keep from worldly strife.
And he thinks a race for riches
  The worst thing in this life.

"Do good," he cried, "with money,
  Ye who have aught to spare,"
And he preaches quite a sermon,
  And ends it with a prayer.

Well! he has bonds with coupons,
  And lots of cash on hand,
And when the fierce Fire Demon,
  Went raging through our land,
The neighborhood was canvassed,
  For money, clothes, and food,
To send the starving people,
  And the man who cries, "Do good,"--

My preaching, praying Christian,
  Now boasts, in pride and glee,
"Those begging, sponging rascals,
  Didn't get a cent from me!
I don't believe their stories,
  About the suffering poor,
The thieves were after money,
  And I sent them from my door."

Oh, out upon such a pretense!
  May a curse be upon his gold,
And the cries of an hundred people,
  Hungry, and naked, and cold,

Ring in his ears forever;
   And the words his false lips pray
Fall on deaf ears in heaven,
   From now till the Judgment Day.

Oh "hypocrites, and liars!"
   Your prayers blaspheme God's name!
And if the angels hear them,
   They blush for you in shame,
And, though you deceive your fellows,
   With the pious cloak you wear;
The hosts of heaven look deeper,
   And they know your true worth there.

DYING.

The great high arch of heaven, like tapestry
  On ancient walls, was grandly colored—save
The quiet, cloudless west, that was a sea
  Of purest crystal—golden wave on wave.
"Oh love," she whispered, "open wide the blind,
  And let me see the glory of the West;
There just across the sea, my soul will find—
  What here is never found—find peace and rest."

Deeper, and darklier grand, the bright clouds grew,
  And red and amber streaks shot through the
    North.
The very light of heaven was shining through
  The crystal West. She reached her thin hand
    forth
And a strange splendor fell upon her face;
  And her dark eyes glowed with unearthly light.
I knew it came from God's celestial place,
  Where there is neither sorrow, death, nor night.

"Oh love!" she cried, "my struggling spirit
    yearns
  To leave this clay and go across the sea,
Look! how to molten gold the whole sky turns;
  And see that white hand beckoning to me.

Oh love, my love, this is not death, to go
   At this sweet hour across the golden tide;
To drop my every care, and henceforth know
   Only the pleasures of that other side."

The angel took the tapestries away,
   And rolled them up in heaven, out of sight,
Leaving the common walls of sombre gray
   To catch the dews and damp fogs of the night.
The west wind played upon his dulcimer.
   I leaned across her couch with bated breath;
"Oh love," I said, as I gazed down on her,
   "Surely, thy words were true, this is not death!"

THANKSGIVING.

Thank God for men! I hear the shout
From east and west go up, and out.
Thank God for men whose hearts are true;
For men who boldly dare, and do.
For men who are not bought and sold,
Who value honor more than gold,
For men large-hearted, noble-minded,
For men whose visions are not blinded
With selfish aims: men who will fight
With tongue or sword, for what is right;
For men whom threats can never cower,
For men who dare to use their power
To shield the right and punish wrong
E'en though his host are bold and strong;
For men who work with hearts and hands
For what the public good demands.
Bless God the thankful people say,
Such men have not all passed away.

Bless God, enough are left, at least
To put a muzzle on the beast
That walks our land from breadth to length
And robs the strong man of his strength,

Takes bread from babes, steals wise men's brains,
And leaves them bound in helpless chains;
Makes sin and sorrow, shame and woe,
Where e'er his cloven foot may go.
This is the mission of the beast
Whose bloated keepers sit and feast
On seasoned dainties that were bought
With blood, and tears, and God knows what.
Keepers who laugh when women cry,
Who smile when children starve and die,
If so they gain one farthing more
To add to their ill-gotten store.

From south and north and west and east,
The people clamored: "Chain the beast!
Fetter the monster Alcohol,
Before he robs us of our all."

Thank God, the earnest cry was heard,
And hearts of noble men were stirred,
And though a weak-kneed host went down
Before the keeper's threatening frown,
Enough were left—a bold, brave few,
Strong-brained, broad-souled men that were true,
Men who were men, and did not fear
The villain's threat, the coward's sneer;
Enough to muzzle with the law
The foulest beast the world e'er saw.
Thank God, thank God, the people say.
True men have not all passed away.

OUR ANGEL.

Upon a couch all robed by careful hands
    For her repose the maiden Mabel lies
Her long bright hair is braided in smooth bands—
    A mass of stranded gold that mortal eyes

May, wandering, gaze upon a little while;
    That mortal hands may touch a few times more.
Her placid lips part in a sweet faint smile;
    And if the glories of that mystic shore

When first they fell upon her spirit eyes—
    All the rare splendor of that unseen way—
Had touched her with a wondering glad surprise,
    And left the pleased expression on her clay.

Her two fair hands are crossed upon her breast—
    Two shapes of wax, upon a drift of snow.
And they have robed her peaceful rest,
    Not in that hateful shroud—that sign of woe,

But in that garb we loved to see her wear;
    A dark blue robe, fashioned by her hand.
I wonder, as I see her lying there,
    If God will give her spirit in His land

Another shape. She could not be more fair.
  I think He will not change her form, or face,
But with the same long rippling golden hair
  She will kneel down before the throne of grace,

And wipe God's feet; and her dark eyes will raise
  Up to Christ's face, and touch Him with her
    hand,
And will with her own sweet voice sing God's
    praise
  And still be fairest in the Angel band.

UNTIL THE NIGHT.

Over the ocean of life's commotion
  We sail till the night comes on.
Sail and sail in a tiny boat,
  Drifting wherever the billows go.
Out on the treacherous sea afloat,
  Beat by the cruel winds that blow,
Hither and thither our boat is drawn,
  Till the day dies out and the night comes on.

Over a meadow of light and shadow
  We wander with weary feet,
Seeking a bauble men call ''Fame,''
  Grasping the dead-sea fruit named ''wealth,''
Finding each but an empty name,
  And the night—the night steals on by stealth.
And we count the season of slumber sweet,
  When hope lies dead in the arms of defeat.

Over the river a great Forever,
  Stretches beyond our sight.
But I know by the glistening pearly gates
  Afar from the region of strife and sin,

A beautiful angel always waits
  To welcome the sheep of the shepherd in.
And out of the shadows of gloom and night,
  They enter the mansion of peace and light.

A TRIBUTE.

My heart that otherwise was glad
   (So much God gives to make it so)
This golden afternoon is sad
   And troubled with another's woe;
And stranger that I am, I fain
   Would send some solace for her pain.

My talks with Sorrow have been brief;
   She touched my robe, in gliding by—
And when I've chanced to meet with Grief,
   He's passed me with averted eye.
Yet, through another's pain, I see
   Sometimes a glimpse of what may be.

And of all griefs that mortals know—
   Of all that pierce the human heart,
There seems to me no other woe
   Like that which rends the soul apart,
When a fond mother sees death's night
   Sealing an infant's eyes of light.

The babe endeared by pangs and fears
　　That she has suffered for its sake,
The babe she watched above with tears,
　　Or sat through lonely nights, awake.
And sang some tender lullaby—
　　And all for this—to see it die.

And thinking of that stricken one,
　　Who weeps to-day a double loss,
Who sees a darkness o'er the sun
　　Made by her overshadowing cross—
And thinking how her poor arms ache—
　　I shed some tears for her sad sake.

Yet in the perfect pure sunlight—
　　In flowers of beauty and perfume,
I think God puts these souls so white,
　　And gives them back to us in bloom.
'Tis thus we have the light and flowers,
　　By yielding up these buds of ours.

In every golden, burnished ray,
　　In every sweet unfolding leaf,
Sad mother, you may find to-day
　　Some little solace in your grief.
God lets them comfort you this wise,
　　Until you join them in the skies.

IN MEMORY OF CHARLIE SPAUL-DING.

Aged 6 years and 5 months; died July 4, 1875.

With eyes that scarce can see for tears,
　We look back o'er the little space
Of baby Charlie's life.　Six years
　Since first we looked upon his face.

Six years since from the angel band
　Our little cherub strayed away.
We did not know or understand
　He was but lent, and could not stay.

We looked into his lovely eyes,
　So large, so soulful, and so deep,
And knew he came from God's own skies,
　And thought that he was our's to keep.

But angels missed him 'round the Throne
　And ere his earthly years were seven,
Christ called him, leaving us alone,
　To turn our sorrowing hearts to Heaven.

For now, no matter what may come,
　Wealth, fortune, honors, earthly bliss,
No place can seem to us like home,
　Hereafter save where Charlie is.

Life could not grow so warm, so bright,
  No circumstances bring such joy,
But that our thoughts each morn and night
  Would turn to Heaven and our boy.

The thought that we may meet him there,
  And walk with him the heavenly plain
Alone can keep us from despair,
  And bring us comfort in our pain.

For Arthur, who is left below,
  Are many thorny paths to tread.
His lips must drink of grief and woe;
  Not so with Charlie, who is dead.

For Arthur there must be, at best,
  Full many an hour of gloom and sorrow;
For Charlie, dwelling with the blest,
  Joy only, through an endless morrow.

Walking the golden streets above,
  He watches o'er us ever more.
God grant through Christ's redeeming love,
  We yet may meet him on that shore.

The thought of death is very sweet—
  The grave can have no chill or gloom
For those who have a child to meet
  Beyond in fields of living bloom.

UNIVERSITY OF CALIFORNIA LIBRARY

Los Angeles

This book is DUE on the last date stamped below.

DISCHARGE-URL

QL OCT 6 1980

SEP 5 1980

4 WK JUN 0 2 1997

REC'D LD-URL
APR 9 1984

APR 8 1984

MAY 1 9 1997

REC'D LD-URL
MAY 6 1985

JUN 0 1 1985

MAR 9 1987

REC'D LD-URL
REC'D CL JUN 1 0 '87

JUN 1 1 1987

REC'D LD-URL

JUL 2 0 1987

REC'D LD-URL

DEC 0 2 '89
LD-URL
41584   JAN 2 7 1989

11343926R00094

Made in the USA
San Bernardino, CA
23 May 2014